STECK-VAUGHN
PORTRAIT OF AMERICA

D0124379

Ohio

Kathleen Thompson

A Turner Book

RSVP

RAINTREE
STECK-VAUGHN
PUBLISHERS
The Steck-Vaughn Company

Austin, Texas

Ohio

Lake Erie

Ashtabula

Toledo

Cleveland

Sandusky

Warren

Findlay

Youngstown

Akron

Lima

Canton

Mansfield

Campbell Hill ▲

Marion

COLUMBUS ✪

Steubenville

Springfield

Zanesville

Muskingum River

Dayton

MOUND CITY
NATIONAL MONUMENT ■

Miami River

Middletown

Cincinnati

Chillicothe

Athens

Ohio River

Portsmouth

Ironton

Contents

Introduction

The settlers who claimed Ohio probably knew the truth shortly after they arrived. Ohio has what it takes to be successful. It's a place with many natural resources, a land of hardworking people with big ideas and important goals. The state's central location and transportation systems connect it to the country as well as to ports in Canada and the rest of the world. Ohio has large deposits of coal, oil, and natural gas. Its rich soil is ideal for growing fruits and vegetables. Ohio has turned out to be the perfect place for people who believe in working hard and dreaming big.

Columbus was chosen as Ohio's capital because its central location makes it equally accessible from any direction.

Ohio

Opening the West

Over a thousand years ago, Native American peoples lived in present-day Ohio. The most well-known are called Mound Builders because they built great mounds for religious ceremonies and for burials. In some burial mounds, archaeologists have found fine pottery, copper ornaments, and stone pipes. Some mounds are shaped like animals. The Great Serpent Mound looks like a snake winding its way along the ground. The entire mound is more than a quarter of a mile long. In southern Ohio there are more than six thousand mounds.

By the 1500s several Native American groups lived in the Ohio region. The largest group was the Erie, who lived along the shores of what is now Lake Erie. The Erie hunted, fished, and grew a variety of crops.

In the East the Iroquois had established trade with the English and the Dutch, trading furs for guns. In the early 1600s, the Iroquois began moving westward as fur supplies grew scarce. As they moved west, the powerful Iroquois began pushing other Native American groups,

The Great Serpent Mound was built by the Fort Ancient Mound Builders almost a thousand years ago. It is the largest animal-shaped mound in North America.

René-Robert Cavelier, Sieur de La Salle, explored the Ohio region. He was a wealthy French fur trader from Montreal.

such as the Shawnee, the Wyandot, the Delaware, and the Miami, out of their homelands. These groups moved west into present-day Ohio and surrounding regions. Eventually the Iroquois moved into the Ohio region. From 1648 to 1656, they attacked the Erie and the other more recently arrived groups as they fought for control of the region.

The French also wanted to control the region. From 1669 to 1670, French explorer René-Robert Cavelier, Sieur de La Salle, explored the Ohio River valley. At about the same time, Louis Jolliet, another French explorer, traveled Lake Erie. Both La Salle and Jolliet claimed the region for France. However, the English had claimed all of the land west of the Allegheny Mountains, including the Ohio region. Both English and French fur trappers were trading in the region. The English became allies with the Iroquois. The French were joined by other Native American groups.

For more than eighty years, the French and the British and their Native American allies struggled for control of the land west of the Alleghenies. Finally, in 1754 the British began attacking French forts in the Ohio Valley. This action began what is called the French and Indian War. In 1763 the French surrendered, and Great Britain took possession of land that stretched as far as the Mississippi River.

By 1775 Great Britain was at war again. This time the British were fighting the American colonists, who wanted independence from Great Britain. Most of the battles of the Revolutionary War took place in the

East. George Rogers Clark, an American military leader, was in charge of the region west of the Allegheny Mountains. He fought several battles in the Ohio River valley against the Shawnee, who were allied with the British.

The Americans won their independence in 1783. With their independence came control of the region west of the Allegheny Mountains called the Northwest Territory. Congress arranged for the sale of Northwest Territory lands in 1785 and planned a system of government for them in 1787. Present-day Ohio is in the eastern part of this region. Settlers began to move into the Northwest Territory almost immediately. Many traveled down the Ohio River looking for land that was more fertile than land in the East. In 1787 a group of businessmen formed the Ohio Company of Associates. The company persuaded Congress to sell them six million acres of land in present-day southeastern Ohio. In 1788 Rufus Putnam of the Ohio Company established Marietta, the first permanent settlement in the Ohio region. The village was located where the Muskingum River joined the Ohio River. In 1789 settlers from New Jersey founded Cincinnati, downriver from Marietta.

The Shawnee Trail, along the Ohio River, is only one of the Native American "roads" in Ohio.

Ottawa Chief Pontiac led a rebellion against the British in 1763 after the French and Indian War ended.

The Miami, the Shawnee, and the Chippewa banded together to fight for their homes. Led by Miami chief Little Turtle, they raided settlements and tried to drive out the settlers. In the 1790s federal troops fought several battles with the Miami and their allies. In 1794 General Anthony Wayne led an attack against Little Turtle at Fallen Timbers, near present-day Toledo. The defeat of Little Turtle gave the United States control of the area that became Ohio.

Settlers continued to pour into the Ohio region. In 1796 a group moving from Connecticut founded Cleveland on the shore of Lake Erie. Other settlers crossed the mountains or came down the Ohio River. The settlers bought land, cleared away the forests, and set up towns and farms.

By 1800 so many people had moved to the Northwest Territory that Congress divided the territory into sections. By 1803 more than seventy thousand people lived in Ohio. That year Ohio became the seventeenth state. It was the first state west of the Alleghenies.

In 1803 the United States purchased the immense Louisiana Territory from France. This land reached from the Mississippi River to the Rocky Mountains. The purchase meant that Ohio merchants and farmers could ship products down the Ohio River to ports along the Mississippi River. Cincinnati became a busy trading port. River travel became easier when a steamboat called the *New Orleans* started sailing on the Ohio River. The success of the *New Orleans* signaled a major change in river transportation.

In 1812 war broke out again between the United States and Great Britain. The Americans had some success holding off the British invasion from Canada. In 1813 Commodore Oliver H. Perry defeated a British fleet crossing Lake Erie. Most of the fighting took place on the East Coast, however. The war ended in 1814 when the British surrendered.

In 1818 a steamboat traveled on Lake Erie from Buffalo, New York, to Cleveland. Great Lakes travel provided another way to move Ohio's goods to market and another way for settlers to move to the region.

This is an artist's conception of Tecumseh meeting William H. Harrison at the Battle of Tippecanoe in 1811. Actually they never met. Tecumseh was one of the greatest Native American leaders. He organized Native American groups to protect their land against settlers.

The *W. P. Snyder, Jr.,* presently at the Ohio River Museum in Marietta, is the only sternwheeler of its type left in the United States. Sternwheelers were used for transportation on the Ohio River in the late 1800s and early 1900s.

By 1820 Ohio had the fifth largest population of any state in America.

In 1825 the Erie Canal was completed. The canal connected cities in New York to Lake Erie. The canal was 364 miles long, 40 feet wide, and 4 feet deep. Settlers used the canal to travel west. Also, the canal allowed goods to travel from Ohio and other Great Lakes states to New York and beyond. Manufactured goods from New England could reach the western farmlands more quickly. In 1826 Ohio began building a series of canals that snaked across the state. The canals allowed goods to be transported between Cincinnati on the Ohio River to Cleveland on Lake Erie.

Ohio's decision in 1835 to include Toledo in the canal system led to a border dispute between Ohio and Michigan. Both states claimed the area, and each threatened to use military force to protect it. In 1836 President Andrew Jackson sent negotiators to solve the problem. Both sides were satisfied when Ohio was awarded Toledo, and Michigan received the Upper Peninsula and statehood.

The state improved its transportation in the 1830s. The National Road, which started in Maryland, reached Columbus in 1835, and railroad construction also began at this time. Locks and dams on the Muskingum River enabled ships to travel all along its length. In 1845 the Miami and Erie Canal connected Cincinnati and Toledo. By the 1850s east-west railroads were constructed across Ohio.

Ohio's transportation system helped the economy grow. Finished products and raw materials, such as coal and iron, were shipped in and out of the state. Ohio's farm crops were sold in distant markets. By 1840 Ohio was a leading producer of wheat, corn, and wool. Cleveland became a manufacturing center. Cincinnati became a shipbuilding center and a major pork and sausage producer.

In the 1840s and 1850s, Ohioans became involved in a political issue being debated all over the United States: slavery. Many Ohioans didn't approve of slavery, so they helped slaves escape to freedom. Runaway slaves traveled on the Underground Railroad, which had routes that ran through Ohio. The Underground Railroad was a system for helping runaway slaves escape by traveling north, sometimes all the way to Canada. People in Ohio and in other states hid runaways in churches and private homes and gave them clothes, money, or food to help them on their way.

Judge Piatt's home in West Liberty was one of the stops on the Underground Railroad. Escaping slaves usually traveled at night and hid in churches and houses during the day.

Some people call Ohio the "Mother of Modern Presidents." Presidents Ulysses S. Grant, Rutherford B. Hayes, James Garfield, Benjamin Harrison, William McKinley, William Howard Taft, and Warren G. Harding were all from Ohio.

Abraham Lincoln was elected President of the United States in 1860. The Southern states disagreed with his views on slavery and the amount of control the federal government had over the states. Eleven states, all of them from the South, withdrew from the Union. These states set up their own nation, which they called the Confederate States of America. The Union North and the Confederate South fought in the Civil War. Although some Ohioans were opposed to the war, the state sent about 340,000 soldiers to fight for the Union. The state also provided materials and food for the Union Army. Union generals William T. Sherman and Ulysses S. Grant were from Ohio.

After the Civil War ended in 1865, Ohio continued to prosper. Agriculture and manufacturing flourished as a result of the state's excellent transportation system. In the 1870s John D. Rockefeller founded the Standard Oil Company in Cleveland. Jeptha Wade combined 12 telegraph companies to form Western Union. B. F. Goodrich opened a rubber factory in Akron. The state's coal mines provided energy for the state's industries. Ohio was booming.

The people who worked in Ohio's factories and mines had a hard life. Often they worked long hours and received as little as five dollars a week. In 1884 miners in Perry County protested by striking, or stopping work. They set several fires in the mines, which continue to burn today. Many tons of coal have already been burned, and attempts to extinguish the smoldering coal have failed.

There had been a few labor unions in Ohio as early as 1830, but after 1880 unions became strong. In a labor union, workers join together and elect representatives to bring their problems to employers. In 1886 the American Federation of Labor (AFL), one of America's largest labor unions, was started in Columbus. In 1890 the AFL organized a nationwide strike. They wanted an eight-hour workday. Even though the strike didn't succeed, unions

Barge traffic on the Erie Canal was essential to Ohio's growing industries. This photo was taken about 1890.

continued to grow.

Ohio industries were growing rapidly, and people moved from the rural areas to work in the factories. In the early 1900s, Orville and Wilbur Wright began building their new invention, the airplane, in Dayton. Their first airplane flew in 1903. Because its location made it a natural crossroads for transportation of iron ore, limestone, and coal, Cleveland became a center of the steel industry. By 1904 Cleveland was a major automobile manufacturing center. By 1910 more than half the people in Ohio lived and worked in cities.

Severe flooding hit Ohio, especially along the Miami River, in 1913. About 350 people died, and more than one hundred million dollars in property was destroyed. In 1914 the state legislature passed a law called the Conservancy Act. This act authorized a system of dams for controlling the Miami River. The project took eight years to complete. The federal government also built dams throughout Ohio.

In 1917 the United States entered World War I on the side of Great Britain and France against Germany. Cleveland and Youngstown increased their production of steel to be used in building war materials. Airplanes were built in Dayton. Lima produced trucks, and Akron produced tires.

World War I ended in 1918, and Ohio manufacturing kept going strong through the 1920s. The Great Depression of the 1930s brought production to a halt. The country's economy was in ruins. Millions of people were unemployed, including almost half of Ohio's workers. Banks and industries across the country closed. In 1932 Franklin D. Roosevelt was elected President. He began a set of programs called the New Deal that put people back to work. In Ohio people built schools, roads, and parks. One Ohio project constructed a series of dams on the Muskingum River. When the river rose in 1937, enough of the project was done to prevent dangerous floods from damaging towns along the Muskingum.

The United States entered World War II in 1941. Once again thousands of Ohioans went off to war. Many other Ohioans went back to work. Again Ohio industries supplied materials such as steel, planes, and tires. At about this time, thousands of African Americans began migrating to Ohio from the mostly rural South. They found factory jobs in the northern industrial cities in Ohio and other states. Ohio continued to prosper after the war ended in 1945.

In 1959 the St. Lawrence Seaway opened. This route along the St. Lawrence River allowed international trade ships to travel from the Atlantic Ocean to ports along the Great Lakes such as Toledo and Cleveland. The seaway made it possible to ship Ohio's products directly to foreign ports.

Ohio's economy suffered in the 1960s. Some industries moved to southern states, where people would work for lower wages. Some steel industries, which had many plants in Ohio cities, began to feel competition from companies overseas. Also, unemployment increased a great deal, especially in the cities.

President Franklin D. Roosevelt's Works Progress Administration (WPA) made jobs for about two million Americans, including these Ohioans. In Ohio many WPA workers worked on the Muskingum River valley flood-control project.

Former Cleveland mayor Carl Stokes is shown here with his family. Stokes was born in poverty in Cleveland. He started working at age 17 and eventually worked his way through college and law school.

The 1960s was a time of racial struggle throughout the United States. The civil rights movement that had started in the South gained national attention. Sometimes the struggle became violent. In 1966 African Americans rioted in Cleveland. Riots also occurred in 1967 in Cincinnati. That same year Carl Stokes was elected mayor of Cleveland. He was the first African American mayor of a large American city. More riots erupted in Cleveland in 1968.

Also in the late 1960s, protests against the Vietnam War grew. Antiwar demonstrations were common at colleges and universities across the nation. At Kent State University, near Akron, the National Guard was called in to control student protesters. During an antiwar demonstration, some members of the Ohio National Guard opened fire, killing four students. The Kent State killings quickly became a symbol of student protest against the war.

In 1971 Ohio instituted an income tax to help pay for schools. Taxes were also used to help solve environmental problems, such as the pollution in Lake Erie. For years industries had pumped pollutants into the lake and the rivers that fed into it. In 1972 Canada and the United States signed an agreement to work together to clean up Lake Erie. The program has taken many years, but it is succeeding.

In the 1970s and 1980s, many people began to move out of Ohio's large cities and into the suburbs. That meant less money was available for city services such as police and fire departments. The state began programs to attract new industries, and the cities began to rebuild and renovate city centers. The programs were successful.

In the 1990s Ohio passed legislation designed to draw new businesses to the state. In 1993 the Cleveland Public Library became one of the first public libraries in the United States to offer access to the Internet. This computer network connects computers across the globe. By using this system, users can search catalogs of libraries throughout the world. Ohio's goals of expanding employment opportunities and information sources are sure to increase prosperity in the years to come.

In Cleveland both sides of the Cuyahoga River are lined with a formerly industrial area called The Flats. Now this area is changing as older buildings are replaced by new restaurants, shops, and apartment buildings.

Dreaming of Flight

Today, we take flying in airplanes for granted. But at the end of the nineteenth century, people could only dream about flying. Two of those dreamers, Orville and Wilbur Wright, made their dreams come true.

In the late 1890s, the Wright brothers had a shop in Dayton, where they designed and sold their own bicycles. The Wrights were more interested in flying than in bicycles, however. Many people were already flying gliders, which are airplanes without motors. Gliders are supported by air currents, which keep them up in the air. The Wrights used the idea of a glider to build a motorized craft that they could control.

The Wrights observed birds in flight. They learned that to control a plane it had to be able to do three things—sometimes all at once. It had to be able to turn right or left, to rise or fall, and to bank, or dip, to one side or the other. The Wrights figured out a way to build a glider that could do those things. Between 1900 and 1902, the Wrights tested several gliders in Kitty Hawk, North Carolina, to be sure they could control flight. Weather conditions in Kitty Hawk were good for flying.

Then the Wrights designed a special propeller and engine. Until then there were only car engines, which were too heavy. Their new engine was lighter. Their niece, Ivonette Wright Miller, remembered how her uncles worked together. "Orville was the one that was bubbling over with ideas.

This 1905 photo shows the Wright Flyer *soaring over Huffman Prairie.*

Orville and Wilbur Wright were the first people to perfect a self-propelled plane. Their invention changed the world forever.

Wilbur was the one who tried to make them practical. They . . . used to scrap a lot . . . You might say they invented the airplane by arguing."

By 1903 the Wrights were ready to test their first powered airplane. They took it to a hill near Kitty Hawk. Their plane traveled down a 60–foot rail before taking to the air. The first flight lasted only 12 seconds, but that didn't matter. The plane had worked! Orville and Wilbur Wright had done something no one had ever done before.

The Wrights returned to Dayton full of ideas to improve their machine. For two years they experimented flying airplanes in a large field east of Dayton. During this time the brothers made 105 flights, many lasting only five minutes or less. The brothers tested their airplanes in New York and even in France. Finally, in 1908 Wilbur flew for one hour and two minutes—a record! Orville and Wilbur Wright's invention started the Age of Aviation. The principles of flight established by the Wright brothers have been used to make airplanes ever since.

Harold and Ivonette Wright Miller are shown with an early aircraft built by the Wright brothers.

Going Strong in the Midwest

Ohio has one of the strongest economies in the United States. That is good news for everyone. When people in the state are making money, they are also spending it. Money circulates within the state and outside its borders. The strength of Ohio's economy is shared by everyone.

Ohio's economy is strong partly because of its transportation system. In 1994 Ohio exported more goods than any other state in the country. Ohio has important ports on Lake Erie and along the Ohio River. The Great Lakes ports take in iron—about forty million tons—and ship out coal. Ports on the Ohio River handle about 56 million tons of freight a year. They carry corn, wheat, oil, coal, limestone, and other building materials. There are also railroad and trucking systems throughout the state. The good transportation system attracts manufacturers to Ohio because companies can easily acquire raw materials and ship their products to distant markets. There's another reason why transportation is important to businesses and

The twin towers of the Proctor & Gamble headquarters grace the Cincinnati skyline. Proctor & Gamble is one of the world's largest manufacturers of cleaning products.

Toledo is an international port that handles more than 14 million tons of cargo, such as coal, corn, and wheat.

A continuous slab caster, such as this one at an Ohio steel-producing plant, can cast sixty inches of steel per minute. Ohio is one of the leading steel-producing states in the nation.

manufacturers. Ohio is close to many markets. In fact it is only six hundred miles from about sixty percent of all the households in the United States.

Manufacturing makes up about 27 percent of Ohio's economy. The state's products bring in over $80 billion every year. The largest portion of this economic activity is transportation equipment—cars, trucks, and aircraft, along with replacement parts. Many automobile plants in Ohio produce various types of vehicles for car companies such as Chrysler, Ford, General Motors, and Honda. Their plants employ about one hundred thousand workers.

Ohio's manufacturing economy is diverse. This means that it produces many different kind of things. For instance Ohio is the second largest steel producer in the country, after Indiana. Ohio companies also produce machinery such as heating and air conditioning systems, ball bearings, and tools that are used to make machines. Other companies produce fabricated metals, or products made of molded metals, such as the metal bases for appliances, motorcycle fenders, and silverware.

This man is helping to assemble a van at a Ford automobile plant in Ohio.

Chemicals, plastics, and processed foods are also manufactured in Ohio. Procter & Gamble produces soaps and other household products. Owens-Corning produces fiberglass and poly-ester products, including specialized cooking and baking utensils. GenCorp makes plastics, especially for use in the aerospace industry. Akron is known for its rubber and plastic materials produced by such compa-nies as Goodyear, Firestone, UniRoyal, and others. Ohio is also the leading glass-producing state in the country.

Ohio is attracting more and more high-technology institutions, such as the Ohio Aerospace Institute in Cleveland.

Mining, primarily coal, makes up one percent of Ohio's economy. Ohio's natural resources have always been one of the state's advantages. Estimates have shown that there's enough coal in Ohio to take care of all of America's energy needs for five hundred years! Ohio also produces about two thirds of the sandstone used in the country. In addition salt is mined in Ohio from the deepest salt mine in the United States.

Agriculture also makes up about one percent of the gross state product, providing about $1.9 billion to Ohio's economy. The state primarily harvests corn and soybeans. Other crops include hay, oats, and wheat. Some Ohio farms are called truck farms. Truck farmers deliver their products directly to local markets. They produce fresh vegetables such as tomatoes, cucumbers, and sweet corn. Farmers in Ohio also raise beef cattle and hogs and produce eggs and milk. Ohio ranks first in greenhouse vegetable production. About 750 acres of crops are grown in greenhouses.

Today, service industries are a large part of all state economies, and Ohio is no exception. These industries make up about 68 percent of Ohio's economy. People who work in a service industry don't make a product or raise crops. Instead they do things for people. The most income produced by Ohio's service economy comes from people who offer community, social, and personal services. This category includes doctors, nurses, lawyers, and people who work in hotels or repair shops.

Retail and wholesale trade is the most important service industry. In retail trade, people sell things to customers. Places such as grocery stores, shoe stores,

Corn is the leading Ohio field crop. More than 15 million acres of land in Ohio is farmland.

and department stores are all retail stores. In wholesale trade, people supply the goods to sell to customers. The most important wholesalers in Ohio handle such items as steel, coal, groceries, and motor vehicles. There are more jobs in wholesale trade than in any other portion of Ohio's service economy.

An average of almost two thousand gallons of wine are produced per day at vineyards in the Lake Erie area. This is an aerial view of Paramount Distillers, Inc.

Financial, insurance, and real estate services are second in importance. Banks are part of this industry, and so are accountants. Most of Ohio's banking businesses are centered in Cleveland, Columbus, and Cincinnati. Real estate involves buying and selling property for businesses and homes. Banks are often involved in real estate, since they lend people the money to buy property.

The government is also part of the service economy. Government workers are employed by the city, county, state, or national governments. Included in this group are people such as teachers, police officers, firefighters, mayors, and garbage collectors. The federal government's part of this economy is mainly the result of Wright-Patterson Air Force Base, near Dayton.

Ohio's economy is strong and getting stronger all the time. The state continues to work hard to attract new industries. This hard work paid off in 1994, when Ohio led the country in the number of new manufacturing plants. With this kind of commitment to gaining new jobs, Ohio's economy is sure to remain among the leaders for many more years.

A Lake Comes Back to Life

Lake Erie is small, as the Great Lakes go. Only Lake Ontario is smaller. Still, Lake Erie is outstanding in its own way. Of all the Great Lakes, it lies farthest south, has the warmest water, and is the shallowest. At its deepest, Lake Erie is 210 feet deep. Parts of Lake Superior, by contrast, lie 1,330 feet below the surface. But small size doesn't mean calm waters. Lake Erie is also the stormiest of the Great Lakes. It is quickly whipped up by winds raging across it from Canada.

For a long time, Lake Erie has been a strong link in the chain of waterways for transport of materials and goods throughout the country. On its United States side, the lake is bordered by New York, Pennsylvania, Michigan, and Ohio. Industrial ports, such as Buffalo and Cleveland, can be found along its shore.

Measured along its curves and bays, Ohio's Lake Erie shoreline runs for about three hundred miles. The Ohio ports of Conneaut, Ashtabula, Cleveland, Sandusky, and Toledo are spread along the lake from east to west. Ships carrying iron ore, limestone, coal, and other cargoes vital to modern industry travel on the Great Lakes to Lake Erie. These ships make stops at Ohio's busy ports.

Until recently, Lake Erie was special in another way, one that people would just as soon forget. By the end of the 1960s, the lake was dying. Its water quality was so bad that swimming was forbidden. Its natural plant and animal life was fast disappearing. The busy transport activity was killing this large body of water.

Wastes from factories, farms, and cities had been polluting the lake for a hundred years or more. Poisons in the wastes, such as mercury, were killing the lake's wildlife.

Another pollution process, called eutrophication, was also at work. Eutrophication occurs when too many nutrients, or nourishing substances, find their way into a lake. Normally lakes support communities of living things that depend on one another. Their life processes advance in a balanced, repeating cycle. Plantlike organisms called algae use nutrients in the water for food. As the algae grow, fish eat them. These fish in turn become food for other fish. When algae and fish die, tiny organisms called bacteria break them down. Bacteria use oxygen in the water to turn the bodies back into nutrients. Then the cycle begins all over again.

But if too many nutrients enter a lake, things can get out of balance. In the case of Lake Erie, the main problem was nutrients called phosphates. These substances came from factory wastes, fertilizers washed from fields by rain, and detergents in city waste water. The algae in the lake thrived on these added phosphates. They multiplied faster than fish could eat them, became too crowded, and died in huge numbers. To break the algae down, the bacteria had to use more

Lake Erie's improvement has not gone unnoticed. Six to eight million tourists visit towns along Lake Erie every year, and the number of marinas, like this one at Put-In-Bay, has increased along the lakefront.

Lakeside factories were the primary source of the pollution of Lake Erie.

and more oxygen. This left no oxygen for the fish. They died, too.

Several species were lost from the lake and its surroundings because of eutrophication and other processes. These species included fish, such as walleye, whitefish, lake trout, and herring, and birds, such as eagles, that feed on these fish.

Finally, in the early 1970s, people woke up to the crisis. Canada and the United States joined forces in 1972 to clean up Lake Erie. To reduce the phosphates entering its waters, Ohio banned detergents containing them. Improved sewage treatment plants were built to remove phosphates from wastewater. Measures were taken to keep other dangerous substances out of the water. For example, farmers began leaving crop residue on the ground, which helps to reduce the amount of erosion into the lake when it rains. These efforts have cost billions of dollars, but they're working.

Without extra nutrients the algae in Lake Erie's waters have decreased, and the amount of oxygen is growing. Levels of poisonous mercury have fallen. Species of fish that had just about disappeared before 1972 have returned. Trout and salmon, stocked in the lake, are thriving. The reproduction rate of fish-eating birds is improving.

The balance is coming back. Lake Erie has been restored to life.

Yet there is still cause for care and concern. Erie's waters and the life they support have changed. The lake will never be the way it was when French explorers first set eyes on it in the 1600s. For example the blue pike, a fish unique to Lake Erie, is now extinct.

Dangerous chemicals still threaten Lake Erie and the other Great Lakes. These include PCBs, which are used in making electronic equipment and pesticides. Some of these chemicals have been building up in lake waters for years. More are carried in all the time by runoff from rainwater. Even the winds carry these poisons to the lakes.

The near death of Lake Erie reminds us how fragile nature is. It warns us to take measures now to prevent future crises. But the revival of the lake gives us hope that we can live in harmony with the natural world.

Cleveland is one of Lake Erie's most important shipping ports. Ships on the Great Lakes unload millions of tons of iron ore in Ohio every year.

The Lake Erie cleanup has made boating and fishing in the lake more popular than ever.

Living in Ohio

One way to discuss the culture of a place is to mention the fine arts that are available. Ohio has symphony orchestras, ballet, paintings, and sculpture. Ohio's crown jewel is the Cleveland Orchestra, which is one of the finest symphony orchestras in the world. Cleveland, Cincinnati, and other Ohio cities also support smaller chamber orchestras, opera companies, and modern and classical dance groups. One group is Cleveland's Dancing Wheels, which features disabled dancers, many of whom dance in their wheelchairs. Dancing Wheels gives 150 performances each year.

In Youngstown the Butler Institute of American Art has one of the best collections of American art in the United States. The Taft Museum in Cincinnati has fine art from all over the world. In Columbus the Wexner Center for the Arts is a leading museum of modern art. The Wexner features a special sculpture by Maya Lin, who was born in Athens, Ohio. The sculpture uses pieces of glass carefully arranged to look like a landscape covered with snow. Maya Lin also

Cedar Point amusement park, in Sandusky, holds the world record for the most roller coasters at a theme park.

The freight barges on the Erie Canal were once pulled by mules. Today, the cargo is tourists!

The Pro Football Hall of Fame is located in Canton, where the National Football League was founded in 1920.

designed the Vietnam War Memorial in Washington, D.C.

Culture also includes the history of a place. Ohio honors the events and people that shaped its history. Seven men born in Ohio went on to become President of the United States: James A. Garfield, Ulysses S. Grant, Warren G. Harding, Benjamin Harrison, Rutherford B. Hayes, William McKinley, and William Howard Taft. Another, William Henry Harrison, made Ohio his home before he became President. All of these men are honored with state monuments.

SunWatch Archaeological Park in Dayton includes a re-creation of a Native American village of one thousand years ago. Near Lebanon is Fort Ancient, which encloses more than one hundred acres of land within huge earthen walls that are more than twenty feet high and three miles long. This archaeological site features evidence of two ancient Native American groups, known today as the Hopewell and the Fort Ancient. The Youngstown Historical Center of Industry and Labor concentrates on the history of the steel industry in the state and the country. Some exhibits are huge steel-making machines that were once used in this industry.

In Toledo a special monument celebrates Admiral Oliver Perry's victory in the War of 1812. The 317-foot-tall monument also celebrates over one hundred years of peace with Canada. In Wapakoneta the Neil Armstrong Air and Space Museum honors the Ohioan who was the first person to walk on the moon. This museum includes exhibits that tell the story of flight, from Orville and Wilbur Wright to the Apollo astronauts.

Groups and individuals have their own culture, based on their history or way of life. People from many cultures have contributed to life in Ohio. Throughout the state there are museums and festivals that celebrate those cultures. The Great-Mohican Indian Pow-wow and Rendezvous features dances, crafts, and storytelling. The Shaker Woods Festival in Columbiana helps people learn more about a special religious community. The Shakers have produced a unique style of furniture, quilts, and other crafts. Ohio's German immigrants celebrate the old ways in the Geauga Lake Old World Oktoberfest. In Dayton the home of the great African American poet Paul Laurence Dunbar has been turned into a museum. It includes a collection of his works and also features programs about his life.

The culture of Ohio is varied and dynamic, homespun and refined. It exists not only as a history of an American people but also as a way of life that is still being lived.

Paul Laurence Dunbar

American poet

10 cents U.S. postage

Paul Laurence Dunbar was one of the first African American writers to become nationally popular. In 1893 he published his first volume of poetry at his own expense. Dunbar worked as an elevator operator. He sold copies of his book to passengers on the elevator.

The Rock and Roll Hall of Fame Museum opened in Cleveland in 1995. The museum is full of music memorabilia, including John Lennon's "Sergeant Pepper" jacket and Roy Orbison's sunglasses.

Strength in Simplicity

In the early 1700s, the first Amish came to the United States to escape religious persecution in Switzerland. In Ohio they settled mainly in Holmes and Geauga counties, where their descendants still live. Over the last one hundred years, their way of life has changed very little. That's because one of the main requirements of the Amish is to live in their own farming communities, separate from the main culture around them. They want to live quietly on their farms, among themselves, following their unique way of life.

Amish culture stresses simplicity. For instance everyone—both adults and children—dresses in plain, dark, "old-fashioned" clothes. Men wear flat-brimmed hats and have beards but no mustaches. Women wear plain long dresses and bonnets. The Amish devotion to simplicity includes more than just clothes. Instead of cars they use horse-drawn carriages. Instead of tractors they use horses to pull their farm machinery. Another way that the Amish keep life simple is to use lanterns instead of electric lights.

In fact the Amish don't use electricity at all. This is one of the ways that they maintain their simple way of life. They don't own telephones, radios, televisions, or other technological innovations. As a result, instead of watching television or playing computer games, family members spend time doing things together. This simple way of family life helps parents pass on the values and traditions of Amish life.

The largest Amish communities in the United States are found in Ohio, Pennsylvania, Indiana, Iowa, and Illinois.

The Amish don't cut themselves completely off from the outside world. For instance when their animals get sick, they call in the local veterinarian. Although they make their own clothes, they may purchase the cloth from a local store. Their communities use most of the crops that they grow, but they sell any excess to people outside the community. In small home businesses, they sell other things, such as handmade quilts, woven baskets, homemade granola, and fresh-ground cornmeal, to "outsiders." There are even Amish restaurants.

For most of us, the Amish way of life, with its carriages and lanterns, may seem old-fashioned. Nevertheless when most Amish children grow up, they stay in the community and continue Amish traditions. It's okay with the Amish if other people don't live the way they do. They just want to be left alone so that they can continue their unique and quiet tradition.

The Amish don't use modern tools or machinery. Work is made easier because the whole community pitches in, such as at this barn raising.

Karamu House: A Special Look at Life

Cleveland's Karamu House is the oldest African American metropolitan art center in the United States. It was founded in 1915 to preserve the artistic heritage of African Americans and to encourage new work by African American artists.

Today, the goals of Karamu House are the same. It has three buildings, all with many special facilities—two theaters, art galleries and studios, dance studios, classrooms, and an early childhood development center. The activities at Karamu House are organized into a number of program centers.

One of the program centers at Karamu House is called the Karamu Performing Arts Theater Center. Every year this professional theater presents plays and musicals that celebrate and explore the African American experience. These plays attempt to demonstrate the kinds of roles African

Langston Hughes, who grew up in Cleveland, is widely thought of as a leading voice of the African American experience.

Every year Karamu House entertains and educates more than 120,000 people of all ages, backgrounds, and levels of experience.

The Karamu Performing Arts Theater Center primarily produces new works by new artists.

Americans have played in history and in the world today. Their topics include issues such as slavery in the rural South, African American pioneers in the Old West, and the political struggles of African Americans in the United States and other countries.

Many of the performances presented at Karamu Theater are of modern plays. But the theater also produces older plays that are a permanent part of African American heritage. For instance Langston Hughes was one of this country's greatest African American poets and playwrights. He and other African American writers brought national attention to African American literature in the 1920s. Karamu House has presented plays by Langston Hughes for more than sixty years. Their latest one is a play called "Black Nativity," a musical celebration of Christmas.

To encourage new playwrights, the theater sponsors Arena Fest, a festival of several new plays. These plays are often produced with nationally known directors in charge. The directors also have special training workshops to help new playwrights and actors learn more about their art.

Other program centers at Karamu House include the Center for Arts and Education. This center offers classes in the visual and performing arts to African Americans of all ages. There are classes in painting, sculpture, acting, and playwriting. Karamu House is important because it not only preserves African American heritage, but it also helps African Americans to express themselves within it.

Looking Forward

Ohio is a state with a strong industrial economy. It has a highly developed transportation system that businesses use to get the raw materials they need and to send their completed products to market. It has rich farmland and ample fresh water. Its coal reserves help supply the energy this country needs to grow.

Ohio also faces many challenges in the future. One of them concerns education. Although Ohio's economy ranks among the best in the nation, many citizens don't share that wealth. This is especially true in its urban areas, where unemployment is high. Ohio is looking at several ways to deal with this problem. One way is to provide the kind of education that would prepare people for high-tech jobs. Specialized jobs that require math, science, and computer skills are becoming more and more common. Ohio is examining its public schools in order to find ways to improve the opportunities open to high school graduates. In addition Ohio's technical schools and colleges are working hand in hand with high-tech businesses. In this way

The University of Akron's College of Polymer Science and Polymer Engineering prepares young adults for future careers in advanced technology.

Preserving the delicate balance of nature in Ohio is vitally important. The Upper Falls at Old Man's Cave in Hocking Hills State Park includes three waterfalls and many sandstone formations.

graduates will be sure they have the skills that they need, and businesses can keep educators aware of industries' changing needs. Policies like these strengthen the quality of life in Ohio for all its citizens.

Another challenge in Ohio concerns the preservation of its environment. Years ago it was normal for industries to dump their wastes in rivers and lakes. That's what caused Ohio's polluted waters. Ohio has passed several antipollution laws, and the improvement is noticeable. Cleaning up pollution is a major effort, however, and pollution still continues to some extent. Ohio faces a challenge to stay one step ahead of the polluters, while continuing to clean up behind them.

Meeting the challenges facing Ohio takes a great deal of dedication. But Ohio has never had a shortage of people willing to tackle challenging problems. That's not going to change now or in the future.

Important Historical Events

1670 René-Robert Cavelier, Sieur de La Salle, is the first European to sail down the Ohio River.

1673 Louis Jolliet explores Lake Erie.

1754 The French and Indian War begins.

1763 The French and Indian War ends with the Treaty of Paris. The land that is now Ohio is given to the British.

1787 Ohio becomes part of the Northwest Territory.

1788 Marietta, Ohio's first permanent American town, is founded. Cincinnati is founded a few months later.

1794 General Anthony Wayne defeats Little Turtle at the Battle of Fallen Timbers.

1796 Cleveland is founded on Lake Erie.

1802 The first ironworking smelter opens in Youngstown.

1803 Ohio becomes the seventeenth state and the first state west of the Alleghenies.

1811 General William Henry Harrison defeats the forces of Tecumseh at the Battle of Tippecanoe.

1813 During the War of 1812, Commodore Oliver Hazard Perry defeats a British fleet at the Battle of Lake Erie.

1825 The Erie Canal is opened.

1832 The Ohio and Erie Canal connects the Ohio River with Cleveland.

1835 A border dispute between Ohio and Michigan becomes known as the Toledo War.

1835 The National Road reaches Columbus.

1845 The Miami and Erie Canal connects Cincinnati and Toledo.

1851 The Ohio legislature approves a new state constitution.

1863 General John Hunt Morgan leads Confederate raiders across Ohio.

1869 Ulysses S. Grant becomes the first President from the state of Ohio.

1871 B. F. Goodrich moves his rubber factory from New York to Akron.

1886 The American Federation of Labor is started in Columbus.

1903 Orville and Wilbur Wright fly the first self-propelled airplane.

1913 Flooding hits the Miami River valley.

1929 The first transcontinental air-rail service in the world opens in Columbus.

1937 Flooding hits the Ohio River valley. Half-completed dams withstand the floodwaters, preventing major disaster.

1955 The Ohio Turnpike is opened.

1959 The St. Lawrence Seaway is opened, making nine Ohio cities international seaports.

1967 Carl Stokes is elected mayor of Cleveland, making him the first African American mayor of a major American city.

1970 Four students at Kent State University are shot and killed by National Guard troops during a protest against the Vietnam War.

1977 Court-ordered busing is instituted in Cleveland.

1988 A major oil spill pollutes the Monongahela and Ohio rivers.

1994 Ohio leads the nation in the number of new and expanded businesses.

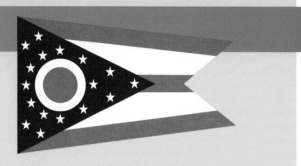

Ohio is the only state with a pennant-shaped flag. There are 17 stars on a blue triangle. The stars are arranged around a white circle with a smaller red circle. The blue triangle and the triangular shape of the flag symbolize the state's abundant roads and waterways. The white and red circles stand for the state's initial. The number of stars represent Ohio as the seventeenth state.

Ohio Almanac

Nickname. The Buckeye State

Capital. Columbus

State Bird. Cardinal

State Flower. Scarlet carnation

State Tree. Buckeye

State Motto. With God, All Things Are Possible

State Song. "Beautiful Ohio"

State Abbreviations. O. (traditional); OH (postal)

Statehood. March 1, 1803, the 17th state

Government. Congress: U.S. senators, 2; U.S. representatives, 19. State Legislature: senators, 33; representatives, 99. Counties: 88

Area. 41,328 sq mi (107,040 sq km), 35th among the states

Greatest Distances. north/south, 245 mi (394 km); east/west, 227 mi (365 km). Shoreline: 312 mi (502 km)

Elevation. Highest: Campbell Hill, 1,550 ft (472 m). Lowest: 433 ft (132 m), along the Ohio River in Hamilton County

Population. 1990 Census: 10,887,325 (1% increase over 1980), 7th among the states. Density: 263 persons per sq mi (102 persons per sq km). Distribution: 74% urban, 26% rural. 1980 Census: 10,797,419

Economy. *Agriculture:* cattle, hogs and pigs, sheep, poultry, corn, hay, wheat, soybeans, oats. *Manufacturing:* machinery, transportation equipment, primary metals, fabricated metal products, electronic and electric equipment, food products. *Mining:* coal, petroleum, sand and gravel, salt, lime, clays

State Seal

State Flower: Scarlet carnation

State Bird: Cardinal

Annual Events

- ★ American-Canadian Sports Show in Cleveland (March)
- ★ May Music Festival in Cincinnati (May)
- ★ Boy Scout Camporee in Greenville (June)
- ★ National Clay Week Festival in Uhrichsville-Dennison (June)
- ★ Ohio Hills Folk Festival in Quaker City (July)
- ★ Shaker Woods Festival in Columbiana (August)
- ★ Ohio State Fair in Columbus (August/September)
- ★ International Mining and Manufacturing Festival in Cadiz (September)
- ★ Jackson Apple Festival (September)
- ★ Woosterfest Community Celebration in Wooster (September)

Places to Visit

- ★ Adena State Memorial in Chillicothe
- ★ Campus Martius: The Museum of the Northwest Territory in Marietta
- ★ Fort Recovery in the village of Fort Recovery
- ★ Kelleys Island in Lake Erie, near Sandusky
- ★ King's Island, near Cincinnati
- ★ Native American mounds and other earthworks: Fort Ancient, near Lebanon; Fort Hill, near Bainbridge; Great Serpent Mound, near Hillsboro
- ★ Pro Football Hall of Fame in Canton
- ★ Schoenbrunn Village, near New Philadelphia
- ★ United States Air Force Museum in Dayton
- ★ Youngstown Historical Center of Industry and Labor in Youngstown

Index